The Nature Kid's Guide to
HAMSTERS

DAVID ANDERSON

LP Media Inc. Publishing
Text copyright © 2026 by LP Media Inc.
All rights reserved.

For information address LP Media Inc. Publishing,
30012 Variolite St NW, Princeton MN 55371
www.lpmedia.org

Publication Data

Hamsters
The Nature Kid's Guide to Hamsters — First edition.

Summary: "Learn all about Hamsters, the Nature Kid Way"
— Provided by publisher.

ISBN: 979-8-89818-236-6

[1. Hamsters – Non-Fiction] I. Title.

Title: The Nature Kid's Guide to Hamsters

CONTENTS

WILD ROOTS

There are over 20 different kinds of wild hamsters — but only 5 are kept as pets!

Whoosh! A wild hamster dashes across the desert sand.

Most people think hamsters only live in cages. Not true! Wild hamsters roam free in many lands. They live in dry fields and sandy hills far from any pet store.

Wild hamsters come from places like Syria and China. Some live in cold parts of Europe too. They dig homes in the dirt and come out at night to search for food.

Pet hamsters still act wild inside their cages. They dig, hide, and stuff their cheeks just like their wild cousins. The wild side never fully leaves!

POUCH POWER
FUN FACT!
A hamster's cheek pouches can hold up to half its body weight — imagine carrying groceries in your cheeks!

Crunch! A hamster packs seeds into its puffy cheeks.

A hamster's body is small and round. It has short legs and tiny ears. Its soft fur can be gold, white, gray, or brown. Most pet hamsters weigh less than a tennis ball.

Hamsters have an amazing trick. They can stuff food into **pouches** in their cheeks. These pouches stretch way back to their shoulders!

Those big cheek pouches help hamsters carry food home fast. You might see a pet hamster stuff a whole treat inside in seconds. It looks so silly and cute!

BURROW BUILDERS

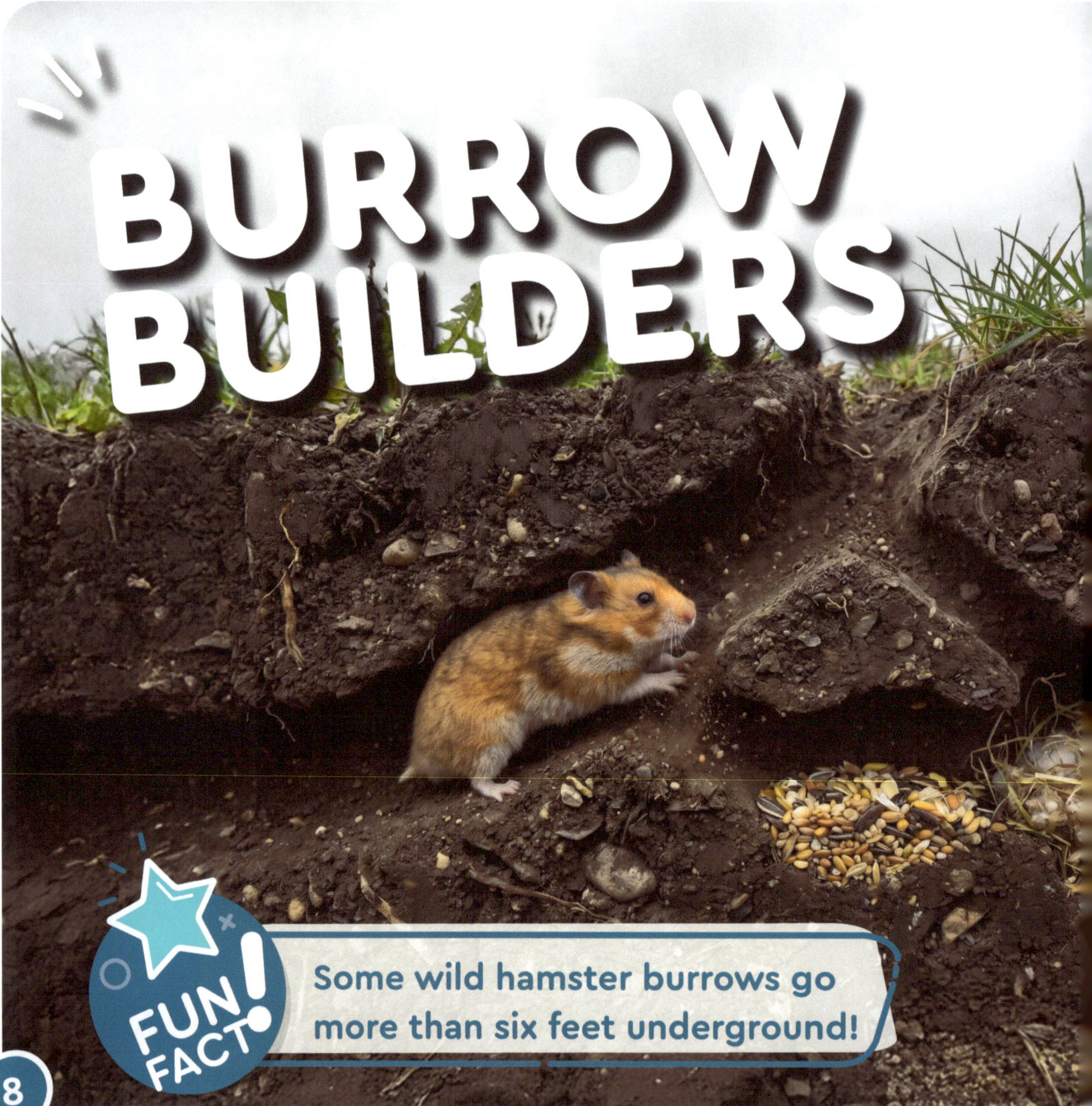

Some wild hamster burrows go more than six feet underground!

Scratch! A hamster digs deep into the cool, dark earth.

Wild hamsters are expert diggers. They make tunnels under the ground that lead to little rooms. Each room has a purpose.

Some **burrows** have many rooms. One room is for food. One is for sleeping. There can even be a bathroom room far from the nest! Hamsters are tidy animals.

Pet hamsters love to dig too. A cage with deep bedding lets them tunnel and hide just like their wild cousins would underground.

MIDNIGHT MILES
DID YOU KNOW?
A hamster can use its whiskers and nose to find its way in total darkness, no light needed!
10

Thump, thump! A hamster races through the dark night.

Hamsters are **nocturnal**. That means they sleep by day and wake up when the sun goes down. Then they are ready to move!

A wild hamster can run up to eight miles in one night. That is like running across 140 football fields! It runs all that way to find seeds and other food.

A pet hamster needs to move at night too. That's why most owners put a wheel in its cage. It lets it run and run for hours! You may hear it spinning in the middle of the night!

WINTER SLEEPERS

Brr! A cold wild hamster curls up into a tiny, warm ball.

Wild hamsters slow down when winter comes. Their body gets very cold and still. This deep rest is called **torpor**. It helps them save energy when food is hard to find.

Before it gets cold, hamsters **hoard** lots of food. They stuff their cheeks and bring seeds to their burrows. Some store many pounds of food underground!

Pet hamsters do not need to sleep all winter. But a cold room can make a pet hamster very sleepy and confused, so a warm and cozy cage is important.

SOLITARY FIGHTERS

Squeak! Two hamsters clash and tumble in the dirt.

Most hamsters like to live alone. They do not want to share their home with anyone. If two hamsters meet, they may fight! They hiss, bite, and chase each other away.

Syrian hamsters want to be alone the most. They will scratch and bite if another hamster gets too close. Even brothers and sisters fight once they grow up.

That is why most pet hamsters need their own cage. One hamster, one cage is the rule — that way each hamster stays safe and happy.

GOLDEN PETS

DID YOU KNOW?

Syrian hamsters can come in
over 40 different fur colors and
patterns — from black to cream
to spotted!

Pitter-pat! A golden hamster scurries to its food bowl.

The Syrian hamster is the most popular pet hamster in the world. It is also called the golden hamster because its fur is often a warm, golden brown.

Syrian hamsters are about six inches long. That makes them the biggest pet hamster you can get. They are also easy to hold and tame, which makes them great for beginners.

A happy Syrian needs lots of room to roam and discover — tubes, tunnels, and a big wheel are perfect for them.

BOLD BURROWERS

FUN FACT!

A European hamster can weigh about one pound — ten times heavier than a Syrian hamster!

Thud! A big European hamster thumps across a farm field.

The European hamster is the biggest wild hamster. It can grow up to 12 inches long — as long as a ruler! Its fur is brown and black with a bright white belly.

These bold hamsters live in fields across Europe. They dig wide burrows with many rooms and tunnels. Farmers sometimes get upset because these hamsters love to eat grain from their fields.

European hamsters are not kept as pets. They are too big and too wild to live in a cage. But they may be the coolest hamsters on Earth!

ROBOROVSKI RACERS

DID YOU KNOW?

Roborovski hamsters are named after a Russian explorer who discovered them in the 1890s!

Zoom! A tiny Roborovski hamster zips across his cage.

The Roborovski hamster is the smallest pet hamster. It is only about two inches long — about as long as your thumb! These tiny furballs weigh less than one ounce.

Robos are super fast. They love to run and zoom around their cage. They almost never sit still, which makes them hard to hold.

Unlike most hamsters, Roborovskis can live in small groups. They do not fight as much as other hamsters. A pair of Robos can share a cage and keep each other company.

CUTE DWARFS

The Campbell's dwarf is the only hamster that can be a true albino — pure white with pink eyes!

Peep! A little Campbell's hamster peeks out of its nest.

Campbell's dwarf hamsters are tiny and cute. They have a dark stripe running down their back. Their fur is gray-brown, and they have fuzzy feet that help them walk on sand.

These hamsters come from the grasslands of Asia. In the wild, they live in sandy, dry places like Mongolia. They are about four inches long — half the size of a Syrian.

Campbell's hamsters can be sweet pets. Handle them gently, and they learn to trust you. A cozy nest box makes them feel safe and secure.

SNOWCOAT SHIFT

Winter white hamsters kept indoors often never turn white — they need short winter days to trigger the color change!

Poof! A hamster's fur turns white as snow falls outside.

Winter white hamsters have an amazing trick. In winter, their fur can change from gray to pure white! This helps them hide in the snow from hungry predators.

These small hamsters come from cold parts of Russia and Kazakhstan. They have thick, soft fur and round bodies. They look like tiny, fluffy snowballs.

As pets, winter whites are gentle and calm. They do well with quiet, kind owners. Talk softly to one, and it will come closer to say hello.

TAIL TRICKSTERS

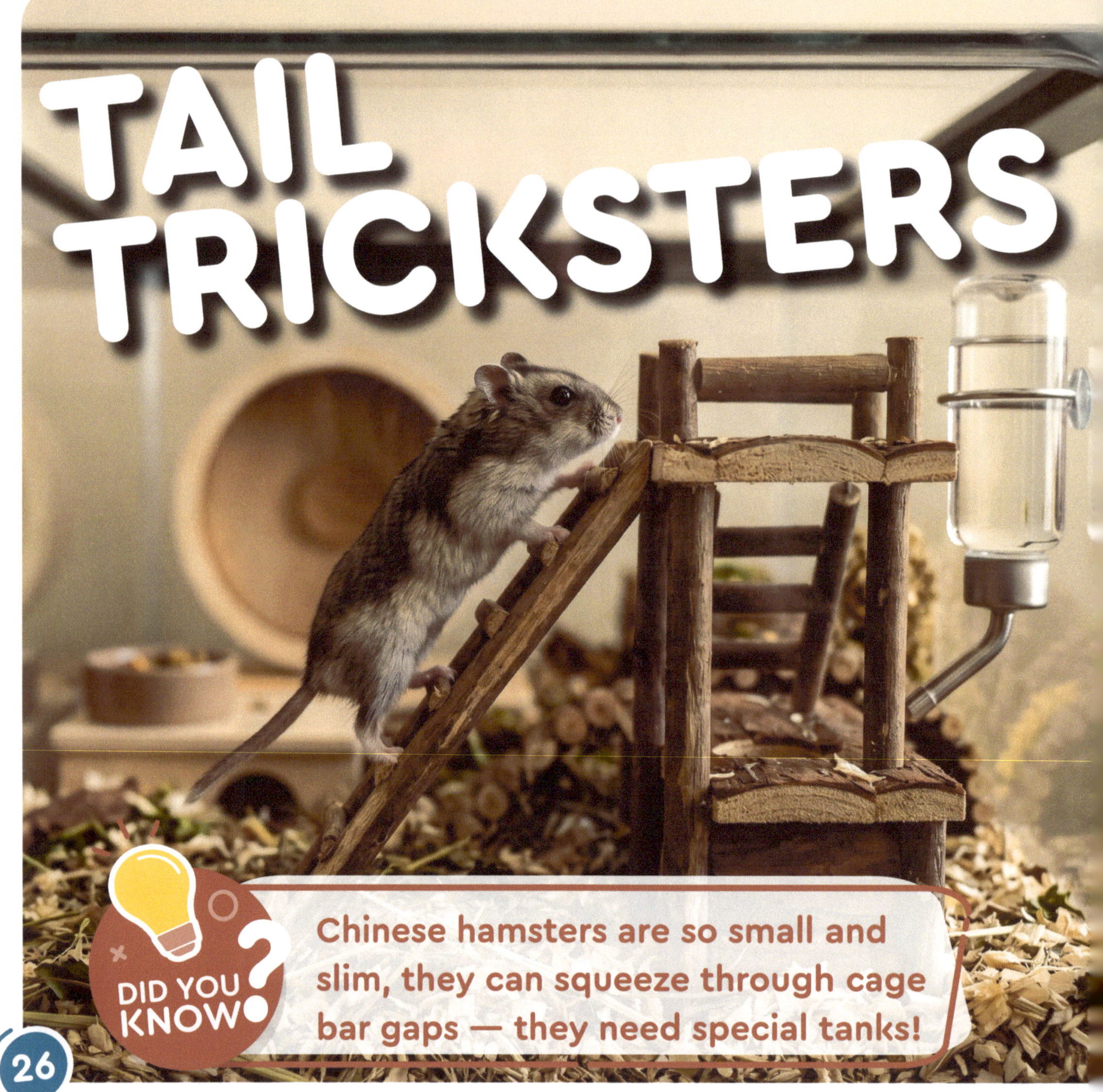

Chinese hamsters are so small and slim, they can squeeze through cage bar gaps — they need special tanks!

Whip! A Chinese hamster swings its long tail as it climbs.

Most hamsters have very short tails. But the Chinese hamster is different! It has a tail about one inch long. That may not sound like much, but it is long for a hamster.

Chinese hamsters use their tail to help them balance. They can grip branches with it as they climb. They look a bit like tiny mice with their slim bodies.

These hamsters are shy but sweet. Give them time, and they will warm up to you. Then they love to sit in your hands and explore your fingers.

GRASSLAND GATHERERS

The greater long-tailed hamster can grow up to eight inches long — tail included!

Rustle! A long-tailed hamster hunts for seeds in tall grass.

The greater long-tailed hamster lives in grassy fields. It is found in parts of China, Korea, and nearby lands. This hamster is bigger than most dwarf hamsters but smaller than a Syrian.

It has a longer tail than most hamsters — about two inches. Its fur is gray or brown to blend in with dry grass. It eats seeds, bugs, and small plants.

This wild hamster is not kept as a pet. But it shows how many kinds of hamsters there are in the world. Not all hamsters live in cages!

HIDDEN
HAMSTER
FUN FACT!
Romanian hamsters look so much like Syrian hamsters that scientists once thought they were the same animal!

Yum! A Romanian hamster nibbles on some grass in an open field.

The Romanian hamster is one you may never see. It lives in grassy fields in parts of Europe, including Romania and Bulgaria. It is small, shy, and very hard to find.

This hamster has sandy brown fur that blends right in with the ground. It digs small burrows and comes out only at night. Even scientists have trouble spotting them!

Romanian hamsters are not kept as pets. Most people have never heard of them. But they play a big part in nature by spreading seeds and feeding predators.

SYRIAN SURVIVORS
DID YOU KNOW?
The first pet hamsters arrived in the United States in 1938 — hidden in a scientist's coat pocket!
32

Peek! A curious Syrian hamster looks out of his glass tank.

In 1930, a scientist found a hamster family in Syria. He dug up a mother and her babies from a burrow eight feet underground. Those hamsters were brought to a lab for study.

Soon people saw how cute and fun hamsters were. They started keeping them as pets. By the 1940s, hamsters were in homes around the world.

Now, millions of kids have a pet hamster at home. Almost all pet Syrian hamsters came from that one family. Your hamster's story started in a burrow in Syria!

WHEEL WISDOM

Whirr! A hamster spins its wheel round and round all night.

A hamster wheel is more than a toy. It is exercise equipment! Hamsters need to run to stay fit and healthy. A wheel helps them do this every single night.

A wheel should be big enough for the hamster using it. For Syrians, that means at least 8 inches across. A small wheel can hurt a hamster's back. A solid wheel with no gaps is safest for tiny feet.

If a hamster runs all night, there is no need to worry! Running helps pet hamsters feel happy, calm, and ready to sleep when morning comes.

VANISHING HAMSTERS

Crash! A tractor plows through a hamster's grassy home.

Some wild hamsters are in big trouble. Farms and cities take over the fields where they live. Without their grassy homes, hamsters cannot dig burrows or find food.

The European hamster is now very rare. It has lost most of its home to farming. Scientists are working hard to help save it by protecting wild fields.

You can help by learning and sharing what you know. Tell friends that hamsters are more than just pets. They are wild animals that need our help too.

FIERCE FLUFFBALLS

A hamster's teeth never stop growing — they must chew every day to keep them short and healthy!

Sniff! A hamster wakes up and stretches its tiny paws.

Hamsters are small, but they are full of surprises. They dig deep burrows, run for miles, fight fiercely, and hoard mountains of food. Every hamster is a tiny wild explorer at heart.

Now you know the real hamster. It is not just a fluffy pet in a cage. It is a tough, smart animal with a big story that stretches back thousands of years.

A pet hamster thrives with space to dig, a wheel to run, and treats to hoard. Watch one up close, and its wild side will shine!

GLOSSARY

nocturnal

Active at night and sleeping during the day.

torpor

A deep sleep that helps an animal save energy.

hoard

To collect and store a lot of food.

burrow

A hole or tunnel an animal digs in the ground.

pouches

Stretchy pockets inside a hamster's cheeks for carrying food.